D0983565

WRITERS' BRITAIN

LIFE AMONG THE ENGLISH

In the same series

British Dramatists Graham Greene
English Country Houses Vita Sackville-West
The English Poets Lord David Cecil

LIFE AMONG
THE ENGLISH

ROSE MACAULAY

with
8 plates in colour
and
22 illustrations in
black & white

PRION

This edition published in Great Britain by Prion
32-34 Gordon House Road,
London NW5 1LP

First published in 1942 by Collins

A catalogue record of this book can be obtained
from the British Library

ISBN 1-85375-231-2

Jacket by Andrea Purdie based on the original design
Typeset by York House Typographic Ltd, London
Colour origination by MRM Graphics, Singapore
Printed & bound in Singapore

BRITISH, SAXON, AND DANISH

OWING TO THE WEATHER, ENGLISH SOCIAL LIFE MUST always have largely occurred either indoors, or, when out of doors, in active motion. The British soon, no doubt, indicated to their Roman colonists that the al fresco life they had led abroad did not do here; they might build piazzas, forums, baths, airy villas and arcades, but to sit about them talking and playing knucklebones and dice was not good enough. 'You can't do that here,' must have been an often heard remark in Britain during the first two or three centuries A.D.

The British parties, at which rich Celtic jewellery and brilliant woad were the wear, occurred first in smoky little wattle and mud dwellings; later, as the populace became urbanized and Romanized, in charming, frescoed, mosaic-tiled villas. Probably parties in the trevs, or forest hamlets, were of a strictly family nature, since other families were viewed with the deepest (and the best justified) suspicion. A firm and somewhat narrow concentration on the family characterized both the Britons and their Saxon conquerors, though a certain amount of non-family social life no doubt took place at religious gatherings, both Druidical and Christian.

The Roman villa consisted of the owner's family, household, agriculturalists and slaves; the former lived in increasing luxury as the rewards of the British export trade grew ever more gratifying, the latter in the discomfort customary among servile classes. The native land-owners ranged from the wealthy, villa-dwelling Romanized British, reared to the habitual use of the Latin tongue, drinking Roman wines and on visiting terms with the Romans in the neighbouring villas, down through the partly Romanized, toga-wearing Celtic chieftains whose wives vainly aped Roman manners, but seldom went so far as to use the fashionable baths in their courtyards and did not really grasp the plumbing system (possibly some Romans, if they at all resembled Romans to-day, did not grasp it either), to the Latinless, bearded, woaded head tribesmen in remote forest clearings, striding among their swine and hectoring their swineherds in Welsh, deeply and fearfully religious, deeply and happily tipsy on mead. The wives of these gentlemen, though doubtless they had their own snobberies, had no Roman ambitions, would have thought it crazy to take a bath, and were much under the sway of their nearest druids.

The city dwellers were a class apart; the social life led by the richer classes in London, Silchester, Uriconium or Bath was of an altogether higher degree of elegance.

A Sea God – a Roman mosaic floor at Verulamium,
St Albans, Hertfordshire.

A Celtic warrior.

These intermarried with Romans; sometimes they made the grand tour to the capital of the empire, returning more Latin than ever. City life was led largely in forum, temple, shops, theatres, and public baths. Visitors from the country were delighted by the delicious foods and wines.

The invading Saxons, a rude and barbarous people, put a stop to all this refinement. Their own social customs were very different; they disliked town life: all the use they had for a town was to sack it and murder its inhabitants. Having successfully achieved this, they settled in the country outside it and built themselves uncomfortable log huts and villages, while the corpse-littered city mouldered into desolation. These rude yokels seldom occupied even the country villas of their victims; these were not the kind of dwellings they cared about or felt at home in; perhaps too they perceived them to be haunted by their slain owners, and thought it safer to keep their distance. Anyhow, they preferred to build timber houses in the clearings, which reminded them of the homes that had so bored them beyond the seas, and in these they settled down to agriculture and hunting. Like the British, they practised family life to savage excess; the social unit was the village community, and dwellers in other villages were rightly suspect; strangers entered the bounds of the tribal homestead at their peril. Such excessive solidarity made social life in some ways very awkward, violent and uneasy.

Within each community, society was elaborately

graded and snob, in the true English manner, sloping down from chieftain and thegns to ceorls, husbandmen, and the unfortunate serfs. A decorative and extravagant people, those who could afford to, wore much ostentatious jewellery, gold cloth and what not, for, though rude, they were dressy, and there was some competition and ill-feeling about this. Masculine fashions in hair were a controversial topic. Saxon gentlemen liked to wear it long (and sometimes to dye it blue); the clergy, after the Christian conversion, preached against this as sinful vanity, as they have in all ages preached against the current fashions of both sexes. Long beards were also for some time the wear, but gradually went out. Ladies went nearly as gay as gentlemen; they wore dresses inconveniently long, but kirtled them up for walking, riding, games, and domestic work. Very busy the ladies were, with spinning the family clothes, brewing, preserving, and ordering their huge households. Immense suppers were devoured each evening in the great hall of the thegn's homestead; those fine eaters, Parson Woodforde and his niece, had nothing on their Saxon forbears as regards appetite. The Normans thought the Saxons consumed unreasonably; their feasts lasted often all night, or from noon till sunset (which shows a pleasant English contempt for afternoon drudgery); the Normans found such conviviality rather vulgar, like other English traits. Never was it the English ideal to 'drink with the duck and dine only once on

'Immense suppers were devoured each evening in the
great hall of the thegn's homestead.'

Saturday.' 'They consumed their whole substance,' says William of Malmesbury, 'in despicable houses, unlike the Norman and French, who in splendid houses lived frugally. They ate till surfeited, and drank till sick.' Saxon social life consisted largely of these feasts, in the timbered hall thick with smoke and rank with humanity, dogs and dirt. (The operations of the housewife and her servants did not include much basic cleaning, though the dirt got covered up with fresh layers of rushes). After supper there were minstrelsy and recitations, till the replete and intoxicated audience rolled off their benches and slept.

Apart from supper parties, the high-spots of social life were probably funerals, which were showy and pyrrhic affairs enjoyed by all. The funeral of thegn or chief was a splendid business of ceremony and flames. The whole village would attend its chief on his setting out for Valhalla or heaven, both before and after the Christian conversion. The effect of this conversion on social life, slight at first, was progressive. The priestly caste gained in status (unlike the Druids, Saxon heathen priests had led rather poor, unrewarded lives, as Coifi, high priest of Odin, remarked), when church and parish developed. Priests, hedged with divine sanctions and versed in mysterious celestial and infernal lore, became a social, spiritual and economic force, disconcerting to land-owners, who had to part with church dues and land, and found Sunday labour forbidden. Their wives

enjoyed worshipping in the grand new frescoed tem-
ples, gossiping with their neighbours after service, and
occasionally going on pilgrimage; they may also have
approved the church's firm line on irregular unions.
The parson became a feature of life, expensive, particularly to the thegn who endowed him, often minatory,
but often also useful, and indispensable for guiding
one's soul into the way of salvation and away from the
shocking eternal perils that he and his church so alarm-
ingly revealed.

Christianity had, too, an aura of fashion, rank, and
cosmopolitan civilization; it had begun here (unlike
elsewhere) as a royal cult, and spread downwards. Snobbery englamoured it; those who still sneaked away to the
old heathen shrines to chant the old charms and slay
oxen for Odin were definitely uncivilized and behind
the times. Some eorls' wives had to admit with mortifi-
cation to their friends (unless they managed to conceal
it) that their husbands still had fits of this old-fashioned
nonsense. Nor were the ladies themselves sure that all
this Christianity was good for the poor. The very slaves
now set up to have souls to be saved; perceiving that
they were on to something good, they crowded to
church, and took full advantage of the new laws against
Sunday work; indeed, if forced by their masters to this
(and really the week's work could not get done in six
days) they claimed the right the new law gave them to be
freed. And though for a time the priests assured their

Norman dress in the 11th century.

flocks that slavery was in order and ordained of God, the thin end of the wedge had certainly been inserted.

As time went on, class differences and snobberies increased. The thegn's position went up, the common freeman's down. The most miserable poverty, the happiest opulence, obtained. A rich burgher class rose, not thought much of by the landed gentry and their wives, but holding the keys of the country's wealth. Before long they had their social revenge, for when the squires were dispossessed by Norman interlopers, the townsmen continued to lead comparatively independent and affluent lives. They saw proud thegns and their families reduced, when not slain or turned off their land altogether, to stewards managing their former estates for the new owners. But the true history of the dispossessed English squires remains to be written, and perhaps never will be, for lack of records. How many turned quisling, how many fled, how many sank into poverty, how many kept their lands as before? Domesday Book, with its list of foreign interloping names, does not solve the riddle.

FEUDAL

THE FRENCHIFYING PROCESS AT WORK ON THE UPPER classes long before the Conquest now rapidly accelerated, though we need not accept sweeping assertions about the sudden and complete mastery and use of French by all who aspired to be gentry, and the relegation of English to ceorls and serfs. Such changes are against nature: the adoption of French as a second tongue, and the more genteel tongue, by the English upper classes does not imply the abandonment of English in ordinary life. It cannot have been only ceorls, villeins and lower tradesmen, or even priests, who preserved and improved the language for two centuries to emerge beautifully as a literary tongue in the thirteenth century. However that may be, Frenchifying continued apace, and the adoption of Norman modes by the gentry widened the class gulf. Walter Map's 'Odit anima mea servos' spoke for many Norman and English minds; the pride of the dispossessed Saxon gentry may well have become embittered into angry scorn. The lady

D i emeral gi' nu balde hm
D a en arabel so ofte bat
O ver teme kerker lac eyn rat
C leyne vñ nich' zu hoch
D aʒ mã in li' vñ vʒ wl zoch
S pise di mã im hiʒ geben
A l nach cristenlichen leben
D isse rede ich nu benyme

A banquet decoration from a 14th-century manuscript.

An Anglo-Saxon Lady from John Strutt's
Dress and Habits of the People of England.

of the Hall, watching her offspring playing about the clearing with the swineherd's children, must have meditated bitterly on the inborn distinctions between her family and theirs.

But the interloping and offensive conquerors, with their interfering and cruel laws, do not seem to have damped English spirits much. The Normans noted Saxon cheerfulness, at the table and elsewhere. 'Nowhere are faces merrier at the board, or hosts more eager to please, or entertainments finer. By nature the Englishman is liberal.' London life was a round of gaiety – football, cockfights, tournaments, ice sports (for, as we know, it froze long and hard every winter in past centuries), fairs, performing animals, every kind of pleasure. *Trop de plaisirs*, said the clergy, as usual; too much finery, too much eating, and far too much drinking. The chroniclers draw a lively picture of the gesticulating, strutting, showy Englishman, always on jollity bent. Rich laity and clergy (and particularly the monastic orders) lived like the fighting-cocks they loved. Social life was largely conducted round the well-spread board, and quarrels were exacerbated by other people's disagreeable table manners and by jealousies as to who could seize the largest helping. Public eating-houses supplemented private hospitality, and if, says Fitzstephen, you arrived at a friend's house too hungry to wait for the next meal, you could fill up the interval at one of these convenient resorts.

Ret chere made our oft to vg everychon

'Social life was largely conducted round the well-spread board'
– a woodcut from Chaucer's *Canterbury Tales*, 1484.

The nation reputed the dressiest in Europe must have spent much on clothes. Rich garments combined with paint, powder and dye to make life expensive, showy and happy, and to enrage puritans. Ladies seem, on the whole to have led jolly lives; having seen to their households and arranged for the next enormous meal, they rode out to hunt or hawk or visit neighbours, attired, no doubt, in all their war-paint. An annual happy occasion for many was going on pilgrimage, either abroad or to Canterbury or Walsingham, riding in gay companies some holy blessed martyr for to seek. In such pastimes, against the grim and bloody background of feudal cruelty, baronial battles, oppressions and re-bellions, royal tyrannies, plague, famine, robberies, bar-barous laws, torture and terror, this cheerful social life ran on.

Education improved. Middle and lower class boys spent bookish, riotous, tavernous and embattled years at one of the new universities; the upper classes, after tuition at home or at some nobleman's house or monas-tic school, often sent their sons on a finishing tour abroad. Clerkly arts, though second to knightly ones, were not disregarded. Girls too learned letters, Latin, and the French of Normandy and Stratford-atte-Bowe – that curious jargon called Anglo-Norman, evolved by a now hybrid people.

The gradual taming of the barons made life (for a time) less war-like, the manorial class more leisured.

The half-enslaved labourers meanwhile lived in hovels, bound to their insanitary villages and to their lord's land, swept by famine and plague. They 'have no penny, pullets for to buy,' but 'a farthing's worth of cockles were a feast for them.' Bitterness spread through the labouring classes; led by a few intellectuals, clerical and lay, class anger found its voice, breaking in 1380 into a revolt that startled the rich into realization of the alarming social problem that rumbled about them. What with the revolt, the clamour for emancipation and high wages, and the blasphemous Lollardry that was getting about, Englishing the Bible and teaching heresy, it was a wonder what the lower classes were coming to; their betters were rightly frightened and disgruntled.

But the gentry had more cause to be nervous of one another than of the poor. Social life in the fifteenth century, as revealed, for instance in the Paston letters, can have had few dull or tranquil moments. Aggressive neighbours lay in wait to seize one another's manors, break into the house, knock the owner on the head, loot his property, and kidnap his lady. 'The world is right wild,' as a friend of the Pastons truly wrote. Between these violent activities, there were sheriffs and jurymen to corrupt (apparently an inexpensive task), manor courts, law-suits, rows in church (one looted the ornaments and assaulted the priest), daughters to marry well, heiresses to kidnap for one's son, hawks and horses to train, games to play, meals to order and eat, all the estate to see to. A full life for both men and women, and if one adjective had to be selected to describe it, perhaps the aptest would be quarrelsome. Private life reflected larger scale wars: neighbours fought, parents and children wrangled in the home. Indeed, children were commonly sent away to be reared (and often married) elsewhere; 'for we either of us weary of the other,' as Margaret Paston wrote of her daughter Margery. 'Weary' seems too mild a word for the emotions which must have been mutually felt by the formidable Agnes Paston and her daughter Elizabeth, while the girl's parents were trying to get her suitably married. To break down Elizabeth's obstinacy (she seems to have been a choosey girl) her mother shut her up and beat her, 'sometimes twice in one day,' until she gave in. It was an unromantic time; girls knew they must marry (or else take the veil), and that marriage was a business proposition; having achieved it, they accepted its obligations, running their husband's house, helping with the estate, bringing up the children with firm bullying, and getting some of their own back out of their lords and masters by giving them elaborate shopping commissions whenever they went to town. Sir John Paston, seems to have meekly obliged, going round the shops with his lady's list of required garments.

Home life was often complicated by a resident chaplain, who, though useful as estate agent, spiritual pastor, and general factotum, was sometimes on difficult terms

English dress in the early 15th century.

with the sons of the house. As, for instance, the Pastons' chaplain, Sir James Gloys; 'the proud, peevish, and evil-disposed priest to us all,' one of the sons called him.

> 'Many quarrels are picked to get my brother and me out of her house. We go not to bed lightly unchided . . . We fell out before my mother, with "Thou proud priest" and "Thou proud squire," my mother taking his part.'

Thus John Paston in 1472, and thus, probably, many other irritated sons of chaplain-ridden mothers. All the same, the chaplain played a valuable part in his patron's secular affairs, and was probably among the more reputable clergy; some of them ran round with poaching and looting gangs and got into the village stocks. More popular were the friars, whose racy preaching and genial manners often endeared them, though contemporary moralists and satirists lampooned them, sturdy patriots disliked their foreign influence, hard-taxed churchmen their mendicancy, and most men their influence over women.

TUDOR

With the stabilizing influence of the rapidly getting richer commercial classes, comfort and prosperity were spreading. There was more tranquility, more leisure, more pleasure, more time for reading, and more to read since printing began. Sir Anthony Fitzherbert, who belonged to the '*trop de plaisirs*' school, complained that noblemen spent twenty times as much on their clothes as they did. As to servants, they are outrageously over-dressed. Dinner parties,

'began with love and charity when a . . . gentleman . . . prayed another to come to dinner . . . and because of his coming he would have a dish or two more than he would have had . . . Then of very love he, remembering how lovingly he was bidden to dinner, and how well he fared, he thinketh . . . he must needs bid him to dinner again, and so ordaineth for him as many . . . such dishes . . . as the other man did, and two or three more, and thus by little and little it is comen far above measure.

And begun of love and charity, and endeth in pride and
gluttony ... '

Play, too, was outrageously high, and often ended in
sorrow.

'One shall lose upon a day or upon a night as much
money as would find him and all his house meat and
drink ... a quarter of a year or more ... it causeth them
to sell their lands, disherit the heirs, and may fortune to
fall to theft, robbery, or such other, to the great hurt of
themselves and of their children, and to the displeasure
of God.'

Still, no doubt they enjoyed themselves.

In such simple and companionable pastimes, then, we
may imagine many a cheerful evening at the manor
whiled away. House games were many – chess, back-
gammon, skittles, shuttlecock, shovel-board (of which
the refined Mr. Strutt, in 1800 or so, writes 'though now
considered exceedingly vulgar, and practised by the
lower classes ... it was formerly in great repute among
the nobility and gentry'), and innumerable card games,
all good for gambling. 'The games of gleek, primero ...
and several others now exploded, employed our sharp-
ing ancestors,' as Goldsmith observed, with what reason
for the aspersion beyond his knowledge of human nature I do not know. Tick-tack and gleek, by the way,

were favourite pastimes of Catherine of Aragon, who was probably, however, not an intelligent or successful sharper.

Sometimes strolling minstrels or players would look in at the manor, but this was not much approved by sober householders, who agreed with the clergy that secular plays were vain, improper and expensive; indeed, the Middle Ages were largely spent in passing laws against them. Sir Anthony Fitzherbert, a wet blanket, thought people had much better go to bed, and not sit up wasting fire, candles and food.

As to reading, it was by no means well thought of by every one. There were always the Squire Westerns who knew that scholars came to no good. Richard Pace met one of these at dinner in 1515, and wrote of him to Colet:

> 'A guest spoke of educating his children . . . There was present one of those whom we call gentlemen, who always carry some horn hanging at their backs, as though they would hunt during dinner. He, hearing letters praised, . . . burst out furiously, "Why do you talk nonsense, friend? A curse on those stupid letters! All learned men are beggars . . . I swear by God's body I'd rather my son should hang than study letters. Gentleman's sons should blow the horn well, hunt, and train a hawk properly. But letters should be left to the sons of rustics".'

When Pace reasoned with him, he drank and changed the subject. But in spite of him education was looking up. Young gentlemen had begun to attend the grammar schools – Eton, Winchester, etc. – and the universities. More important, however, were polite table manners. Innumerable etiquette books reveal our ancestors at food. They are admonished not to fill their mouths so full that they cannot hold them shut while chewing, not to pick their noses or blow them on their napkins, but '*If thou must spit or blow thy nose, keep thou it out of sight, let it not lie upon the ground, but tread thou it out right,*' not to pick the teeth with knife or fingers, but with stick or wand, not to return bitten food to the dish, spit over the table or into the finger bowl, bring cats to meals, scratch, or speak offensively to those present or about those absent. A great ideal: how far our ancestors lived up to it is not for us to say; possibly no better than we do today.

According to the Venetian ambassador here in 1500 (or his secretary) the English, though consumed with irrational patriotism and some (probably less irrational) xenophobia, were excellent hosts. Both gentlemen and ladies frequented taverns, those ancient centres of social life. As Lyly later made his old Elizabethan gentleman remark, 'A tavern is a rendezvous . . . for good fellows. I have heard my great grandfather tell how his great grandfather should say that it was an old proverb when his great grandfather was a child' (which gets us back to about Magna Carta) 'that it was a good wind that blew a man to the wine.' As to water, 'it was good to drink when men did eat acorns,' to quote an Elizabethan dinner-party phrase.

The English, said our Italian diplomat, are civil, and dress finely. Offering a foreigner some delicacy, they ask him if it is to be had in *his* country, which sounds like a modern Russian. There are divers religious opinions. Lollardry was troublesome again; so were modernism and the new learning: perhaps the Italian met diners like Piers Plowman's 'high men eating at table,' who, when 'at meat in their mirth when minstrels be still,' would tell of the Trinity a tale or twain; or perhaps he had seen belated Lollards burnt at Smithfield. Anyhow, his observation here seems shrewder than when he looked for signs of love in Englishmen, and failed, as other Italians have failed, to observe any. The women, however, he thought violent in their passions, which looks as if he had got on pretty well. Their children English parents do not love at all; they send them from home, so that they shall not share in the food.

As the lavish Tudor century rolled on, social occasions increased in exuberance. Here is Miles Coverdale complaining of bride-ales:

'Early in the morning of the wedding people begin to exceed in superfluous eating and drinking ... They go from the church light, nice, in shameful pomp and vain

Banquet dancing at Moreton Hall in Cheshire *c.* 1500.

wantonness. After the banquet ... the bride must be brought into an open dancing place. Then there is such a running, leaping and flying among them; then there is such a lifting up of the damsel's clothes and of other women's apparel, that a man might think all these dancers ... were become stark mad ... and that noise and rumbling endureth even till supper. As for supper, look how much shameless and drunken the evening is more than the morning, so much the more vice, excess, and misnurture is used at the supper.'

All table manners forgotten, obviously.

'And though the young persons (being weary of the babbling noise and inconvenience) come once towards their rest, yet can they have no quietness. For ... unmannerly and restless people ... go to their chamber door, and there sing vicious and naughty ballads ... '

This was perhaps overdoing a party of pleasure. Let us hope (as Strutt says kindly about Stephen Gosson's criticisms of the low behaviour of Elizabethan theatre audiences) that Coverdale was acquainted with vulgar wedding parties only, or was exaggerating. Few amusements emerge with a good reputation from the pens of clerical scribes; even May Day celebrations wear an orgiastic, bacchanalian air. Herrick, himself something of a Bacchus, was almost the first clergyman to make them sound innocent.

Extravagant royal romps and pomps set the fashion, as the magnificent Henry VIII followed his thrifty parent. The nobility were badly out of pocket with it all. The poor meanwhile enjoyed the shows free. Progresses, processions, pageants, puppet shows, fairs, jugglers, dwarfs, dancing monkeys, baited bears and bulls, executions, a mad preacher, a man at the cart's tail, a woman with two heads – anything to stare at did. And, for rich and poor, any sport or game.

With the Renaissance secularization of thought, the pastime of travel changed its basis from pilgrimism to tourism. The wife of Bath had got about the world; she had visited Jerusalem, Rome, Boulogne, Cologne, and Spain. She had a much better time than her sex did in the sixteenth century; but for young gentlemen secular travel became the mode; it was believed to polish them. So abroad the young gentlemen went, gallivanting about France and Italy, and sour critics grumbled that they came back worse than they went, having learnt 'atheism, vicious conversation, ambitious and proud behaviour,' and to stroll about with pages at their heels, sneering at virtue. Whether our tourists actually suffered such detriment, and were so different from tourists to-day, we cannot pronounce; perhaps those who said so were merely jealous. Travellers themselves took a more favourable view; that ardent Elizabethan tourist, Thomas Coryat, opined that stay-at-homes were apt to be 'rude, slothful, rough, outrageous, foolish, barbarous

. . . also effeminate, wanton, given to sleep, banquetings, dice and idleness . . . and the enticements of all concupiscences' – all the things, in fact, of which the stay-at-homes accused the tourist. Whichever was right, if either, the sixteenth century certainly brought tourism into fashion.

Money changed hands quickly, as the new nobility ousted the old, the rewards of commerce enriched the merchants, and monastic plunder the courtiers. Both ladies and gentlemen chased the fashions with avidity. Ascham complained, thinking it silly:

'Some new disguised garment or desperate hat, fond in fashion or garish in colour, whatsoever it cost, however small his living be, . . . gotten it must be, and used with the first, or else the grace of it is stale and gone.'

And the learned and reverend William Harrison:

'Except it were a dog in a doublet, you shall not see any so disguised as are my countrymen . . . How curious, how nice are a number of men and women, and how hardly can the tailor please them in making it fit for their bodies! How many times must it be sent back to him that made it!'

As to ladies, they kept up with gentlemen. In fact,

Lord Darnley.
Gemahl der Königin Maria v. Schottland
1566.

Marquise von Dorset.

Königin Maria v. Schottland.
1566.

Mary Queen of Scots and Lord Darnley in English
court dress *c.* 1566.

A family at leisure *c*. 1500.

'They do far now exceed the lightness of our men, and such staring attire as in time past was supposed meet for ... light housewives only, is now become a habit for chaste and sober matrons. What shall I say of their doublets, ... their galligascons to bear out their bums ... I have met with some of these trulls ... so disguised that it passed my skill to discern whether they were men or women ... '

The only class more soberly attired than of old were the clergy, both Protestant and Catholic. Priests formerly, according to Harrison, must have presented a charming appearance, for they

'went in garments of light hue ... with their shoes piked, their hair crisped, ... their apparel ... of silk and richly furred, their caps laced with gold, so that to meet a priest in those days was to behold a peacock that spreadeth his tail when he danceth before the hen, which now (I say) is well reformed.'

Whether over-eating was also well reformed or not, Harrison is doubtful, though meals were fewer,

'for whereas of old we had breakfasts in the forenoon, beverages or nunchions after dinner, and rear suppers generally when it was time to go to rest ... now these odd repasts, thanked be God, are very well left, and each one (except here and there some young hungry stomach that cannot fast till dinner time) contenteth himself with dinner and supper only.'

Actually, breakfast (beer and manchets) seems to have been common too. Dinner (among gentry) was about eleven, supper about six. Merchants ate slightly later, husbandmen later still; the poorest sort when they could. Meals were still heavy.

> 'In number of dishes . . . the nobility of England (whose cooks are for the most part musical-headed Frenchmen) do most exceed, since, no day passeth . . . wherein they have not only beef, mutton, veal, lamb, kid, pork, cony, capon, pig, . . . but also some portion of the red or fallow deer.'

Fine dinner services, silver, and Venice glass set off this fine eating.

Houses were more luxurious; window glass and more chimneys came in. Some thought this did the health no good. 'Now have we many chimneys, and yet our tenderlings complain of rheums.' They complained too of plague, though houses had grown less dirty since Erasmus had been disgusted with them. But plague mainly afflicted the poor, whose houses and persons were doubtless as dirty as ever.

Class barriers remained high, though they could be o'erleaped. There were first the nobility; then the esquires born; then those who, though 'their ancestors were not known to come in with William of Normandy,' became gentry from following the liberal professions or

An Elizabethan picnic – a woodcut from
G. Turberville's *Book of Venerie*, 1572.

serving as captains in the wars, had arms bestowed on them, and were thenceforth called 'master,' and 're-puted for a gentleman ever after.' Then the burgesses, who 'often change estate with gentlemen . . . by mutual conversion of one into the other;' then the yeomen, called not 'master' but 'goodman.' Below these stret-ched 'the vulgar and common souls,' small tradesmen, peasants, the town rabble who so disgusted foreigners by their rude xenophobia, shouts of 'French knave! Whore's son!' and throwing of cabbages.

Foreigners' comments are interesting, if occasionally shallow. They noticed that Englishwomen have ten husbands each, that Englishmen have tails, and the Scotch black faces. They noted also our luxury, fine dressing and eating, religious opinionism, little interest in literature or soldiering, strong addiction to games, sport, the drama, and the baiting of the larger mammals. Women 'have far more liberty than in other lands, and know how to use it,' for they go about freely without their husbands (these are less jealous than continental husbands, no doubt because Englishmen do not love). Women enjoy taverns; if you invite a lady friend there to take wine and sugar, 'then she will bring three or four other women along, and they gaily toast each other; the husband afterwards thanks him who has given his wife such pleasure.'

On the whole, sixteenth century women managed to put in a pretty good time. Here is a Dutch view:

'They are well dressed, fond of taking it easy, and commonly leave household matters and drudgery to their servants. They sit at their doors, in fine clothes, to see and be seen of the passers by ... They spend their time walking, riding, visiting their friends, making merry with them at childbirths, christenings, church-ings and funerals. .... This is why England is called the paradise of married women.'

Some ladies,

'lie till nine or ten every morning, then, being roused forth of their dens, they are two or three hours in putting on their robes, which being done they go to dinner, where no delicacies ... are wanting. Then, their bodies satisfied and their heads prettily mizzled with wine, they walk abroad for a time, or else confer with their familiars, as women, you know, are talkative enough, and can chat like pies, all the world knoweth it. Thus some spend the day till supper time, and then the night as before.'

As to gentlemen,

First, he doth rise at ten, and at eleven
He goes to 'Gyls,' where he doth eat till one;
Then sees a play till six, and sups at seven;
And after supper straight to bed is gone;
And there till ten next day he doth remain;
And then he dines, and sees a Comedy,

And then he sups and goes to bed again:
Thus round he runs without variety.

Obviously a drama fan. But every Elizabethan except the puritans was this. The playhouse was the fashionable gentry's diversion, the apprentice's recreation, the intellectual's art, the performer's livelihood, the puritan's bugbear, the town's talk. People flocked to the theatre to pass an afternoon, to see a play, to meet one another; and a pretty good time the audience had, apart from the play, if we are to believe that very disagreeable clergyman, Stephen Gosson:

'Such heaving and shoving, such itching and shouldering to sit by women; such care for their garments, that they be not trod on; ... such pillows to their backs ... such giving them pippins to pass the time ... such tickling, such toying, such smiling, such winking, and such manning them home when the sports are ended ...'

And such pickings up, too, for

'every wanton and his paramour, every man and his mistress, every John and his Joan, every knave and his quean, are there first acquainted.'

Gosson, like other puritans, took the low view of his neighbours and their recreations. Practically all social

The Laughing Audience – an engraving by
William Hogarth, 1733.

activities – playgoing, masques, wedding and christening parties, funeral wakes, maying, even paying calls, even promenading in Paul's Walk, all the innocent and happy amusements of mankind, and particularly making love, they viewed with apprehension and disdain.

They seldom, however, had much effect on mankind, and social activities ran their cheerful course, regardless of the sneers of the precisians, which were repaid with interest.

A fine example of extravagant pleasuring was set by the queen, and followed by her subjects; till Gloriana, having gone far to ruin many of them, as she had enriched others, made at last a handsome exit, and the magnificent Tudor century eased off into the less grandiose and flamboyant Stuart period.

'Extravagant royal romps and pomps set the fashion.'
– Queen Elizabeth at Tilbury, 1588.

STUART

WE SLIDE WITH THE SEVENTEENTH CENTURY, INTO A gentler, less rampageous age; socially more civilized, intellectually less at the boil but more adult. The brilliant, crude, questing, adventurous hoyden becomes quieter, duller, better mannered. The Jacobeans and Carolines are an epoch nearer to us in spirit. Dorothy Osborne, in the mid century, might have been a Jane Austen heroine. The educated puritan country gentry, the Verneys, Hutchinsons, Hampdens and their friends, speak our language (unlike the vituperating extremists, the Prynnes, Bastwicks, and 'saints,' who speak a strange tongue of their own). The Anglican country parson emerges, the achieved creature of the Anglican compromise, sometimes the sober, kindly (and often scholarly or poetic) minister and friend of his people, sometimes the toady of squire or bishop, sometimes the scandalous neglecter of his duties of whom Laud and Milton (from opposite angles) complained. Village life revolved round him and round the small squire, who was developing too, becoming, with the break up of many of the larger estates, more important, often M.P. as well as J.P., politically self-confident (as Charles I was soon to find), a baiter of bishops, thinking most of them High Church and low born. But he still pursued animals, saw to his lands, rode to market and shire court, quarrelled with his neighbours, and genially patroned the country round of pleasurings, from Twelfth Night wassailings to Rogation processions, Whitsun ales, harvest homes, All Hallows E'en, and Christmas mummings.

There were attempts, supported by some squires and clergy, but firmly opposed by the Crown (which liked to spite the puritans), and by most people (who liked diversion), to make Sunday a dull day. The Book of Sports shows how people actually spent Sunday afternoons, enacting that those who had attended morning church (but not those who hadn't) should enjoy in the afternoon 'harmless recreation,' only not bear and bull baiting, interludes, or, in the case of the meaner sort of people, bowls. (Bowls were apparently class, and put the poor above themselves if they indulged in them, Sundays or week-days). Country life can never (*pace* Herrick) have been dull, to those who enjoyed any form of outdoor sport and were not prigs demanding intelligent society.

As to the more intellectual gentry (and the stupid unlettered squire who had a century ago shocked Dr.

Pace at dinner was growing rarer, except in far outposts of north and west; most of his class now had a book or two lying about the house, and many collected fine libraries) – as to the intellectual gentry, they were apt to meet and talk about philosophy, literature and politics in some country house, as Lord Falkland and his friends did at Great Tew. Highbrow gatherings came into fashion, and country houses were often clearing-houses for the political, ecclesiastical, theological and literary problems that disturbed thoughtful gentlemen. 'The studies in fashion those days in England,' says Aubrey, 'were poetry, and controversy with the church of Rome.' Lord Falkland's gatherings at Great Tew neglected, we may be sure, neither of these engaging topics. 'His house was like the University itself for the company that resorted there.' Scholars, wits, poets, theologians, professors of Greek, assembled and chattered about Shakespeare's place in literature, the relative merits of contemporary poets, the relations of church, state and crown, the limits of knowledge, any interesting subject that came up; they were more scholarly and rational, though probably less hilarious, than the literary and Bacchic Jonsonian symposia at the taverns, 'those lyric feasts' of the 'twenties. Good talk must always have been a social object, but in this century it assumes greater prominence. There were hostesses like old Lady Falkland, who 'loved good company so much that the contrary was insupportable to her.' Table talk and *bon mots* were collected, and, as Clarendon records of Edmund Waller, his wit and pleasantness of conversation was 'enough to cover a world of very great faults,' so that 'his company was acceptable where his spirit was odious.'

Good company was naturally, then as always, more accessible in town than country. Londoners could meet in Paul's Walk in the mornings and 'walk and talk in the middle aisle ... The noise is like that of bees ... It is the great exchange of all discourse ... the general mint of all famous lies' – and go from thence to attend a play, see a cock-fight, or take a hackney coach from the Maypole in the Strand to visit friends. One could play paille maille in the street appointed for it, or bowls in a bowling alley, or take a boat or barge up the river to Chelsea or down the river to Deptford to have a drink on Drake's Golden Hind. Musical water parties were fashionable; so was driving a coach to some village, supping, dicing and courting there, and returning in the long summer evening before highwayman time.

Ladies joined in most of these recreations (often masked); they taverned less than in the last century; but were still more ardent play-goers, and passionate masque addicts. Games, both indoors and out, were continual; much money changed hands over them, and to be ruined at cards, dice, or (as with Sir John Suckling) bowls, was common in both sexes; when Suckling played bowls in Piccadilly, his sisters stood by crying for

The Cockpit

fear he should lose their portions as well as his own. But, to do Sir John justice, he enriched himself by £20,000 at cribbage, by means (says Aubrey) of marking the cards. Gentlemen and ladies used to consult their astrologers as to when to stake high, for then, as now, astrology was a fashionable cozenage.

As always, all popular pastimes were attacked by the professional kill-joys – once the pre-Reformation preachers, now their heirs, the puritans. These, their hatred of communal pleasures growing more passionate with the years, and with the baiting they got from the ordinary man, attacked practically all social gaiety, with bitter emphasis on entertainments popular at court. Court life under James I was pretty gluttonous, intemperate and vicious; excessive enthusiasm about supper sometimes upset both table and food; and the deep gobbling and drinking that went on were fair game for the precisians. But these disliked still more the lovely entertainment of masques, now reaching fantastic exquisiteness and absurdity. There were the prettiest and most extravagant transformation scenes, the most elegant oceans with heaving billows, lit scallop shells bearing the dramatis personae to dance on wooded shores, singing mermaids, river-gods, tritons, everything suitable to marine pantomime. It was an amusement expensive, delightful, fashionable, and detestable to disapprovers. The two first Stuart queens adored it, and sometimes performed in it, and female performers shocked puritans even more than males; though in 1634 a girl of the best family was acting in a masque written for her by a puritan poet.

The lavishness and coarseness of the Jacobean court was fined down under Charles, a puritan himself in morals. Charles was a prig: not so his lively French wife, whose goings on and foreign *entourage* immensely annoyed the puritans and cost Prynne his ears. Under Henrietta, Roman Catholicism became fashionable, and conversions among court ladies raged.

Many of the best people preferred not to come to court, but to lead quiet lives on their estates – that country life of which dissipated young Tom Verney said 'Rather than lead this hellish life, I will take a rope and make an end of myself.' The average young gentlewoman had no choice; she stayed at home, and amused herself with such pursuits as offered, if she found time for amusement between her duties in the house, for her mama, formidably busy with housewifery, required her assistance. As also her obedience. A nice and properly behaved young woman wrote of her mother, 'As long as she lived, I do not remember that I made a visit to the nearest neighbour or went anywhere without her liberty.' This young lady was full of nice feelings. She goes on,

'So scrupulous was I of giving any occasion to speak of me as I know they did of others, that, though I loved

A contemporary engraving of a London coffee house *c*. 1700.

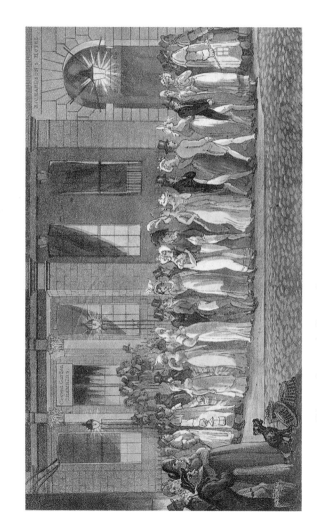

Riotous dancers in Covent Garden are taken to the watch-house
– an engraving by Thomas Rowlandson, 1821

well to see plays and to walk in the Spring Garden sometimes (before it grew scandalous by the abuse of some) yet I cannot remember three times that ever I went with any man besides my brothers ... And I was the first that prepared and practised three or four of us going together without any man, and every one paying for themselves ... And this I did first upon hearing some gentlemen telling what ladies they had waited on at the plays, and how much it had cost them; upon which I resolved none should say the same of me.'

There was just then a bevy of rather priggish, proper, and quietly studious young ladies, who took to their books like ducks to water (nothing could drag Lucy Hutchinson from them, and she would pull her little friends' dolls to pieces). Some girls got a good education from the family tutor, others never learned even remotely to spell English or any other tongue. Some were 'hoyting girls' who only loved games and sport and running wild with their brothers; some enjoyed themselves beyond the limits of propriety with the other sex; others were good young creatures who obeyed their parents, married as bidden, and produced fifteen children; some were bluestockings, some pious, some wits. No other half century has left us so many memoirs and autobiographies by women, or more fond connubial letters. Preference now played more part in marriages, parental arrangement rather less. Dorothy Osborne, writing to her lover in 1653, enumerates the qualities

she must find in a prospective husband, with a firmness that would have enraged Paston parents and amazed their daughters.

'He must have that kind of breeding that I have had, and used that kind of company, that is, he must not be so much a Country Gentleman as to understand nothing but hawks and dogs and be fonder of either than of his wife, nor of the next sort of them, whose aim reaches no further than to be Justice of the Peace and once in his life High Sheriff . . . He must not be a thing that began the world in a free school, was sent from thence to a university, and is at his furthest when he reaches the Inns of Court . . . he must not be a Town Gallant neither, that lives in a Tavern and an Ordinary, that cannot imagine how an hour should be spent without company unless it be in sleeping . . . Nor a Travelled Mounsieur whose head is all feathers within and without, that can talk of nothing but dances and duels . . . he must not be a fool of no sort, nor peevish nor ill-natured nor proud nor coveteous. . . . '

(A catalogue that indicates that the Puritan Commonwealth had not had much effect on English social types). Still, as Peacham expressed it a quarter of a century earlier, if a girl lacked a good portion, 'she may live till she be as old as . . . the nurse of Æneas ere you shall get her a good match.'

There were then, as now, a hundred different Englands. Through one recorder's eyes we see frivolous court-goers, scent-soaked, ornament-hung, wearing little mirrors in their hats, crowding round gaming tables and drink bars, furnishing texts for puritan invective; through another's, quiet, well-bred, thoughtful country squires like the Verneys, the people on whom John Evelyn looked nostalgically (and perhaps inaccurately) back in his old age at the end of the century –

'In those happy days Surefoot, the grave and steady mare, carried the good knight and his courteous Lady behind him to church, and to visit the neighbourhood, without so many hell-carts, rattling coaches, and a crew of damme lackeys.'

Young ladies, added the old gentleman, span more in those good days and disdained not the needle, nor read so many romances, nor saw so many plays and smutty farces; at Christmas they were diverted by honest gleek, ruff, and other games. Aubrey, whose view of his fellow creatures was other, would have said that the young ladies (and gentlemen too) played these games for immense sums, and sharped at them as best they could.

There were country gentry like these, a few like the civilized and highbrow Falkland and his friends, more, no doubt, like him whom Dorothy Osborne rejects, and of whom (the type persisting through all political changes), the feminist Mary Astell wrote in the 1690's – 'His conversation is wholly taken up with his horses, his dogs

52

Hunting the Hare – a drawing by Francis Barlow, 1626–1702.

and hawks, his entertainment is stale beer.' But in the main these often derided beings seem to have been sensible and steady enough, influential locally, increasingly pulling their political weight, putting their younger sons into law or trade, enthusiastically or reluctantly mustering their tenant troops for king or parliament when that long quarrel at last broke, fighting to the bitter end, usually ruined, plundered and sequestrated, and (if they were king's men) often exiled till they returned at the Restoration to their dwindled estates to beg compensation in vain. It was not of these, but of the town gallants, that Peacham complained, 'We, the apes of Europe, like Proteus, must change our shapes every year, nay, quarter, month and week,' The country gentry only mildly followed the fashions; their chief sartorial extravagance seems to have been indulgence in excessive mourning; Sir Ralph Verney, when widowed, set himself up not only with black suits, but black nightclothes, nightcaps, slippers, bed, brush and comb (and probably toothbrush, these implements having lately come in) and carriage.

The cleavage that split the nation into two camps was good for neither, and made both self-righteous, contemptuous and abusive. The 'intruded' puritan clergy were not popular. Mary Verney (a mild puritan of the country gentry type) complained that the voice of the new clergyman 'made every one laugh.' Evelyn called them briefly 'the canters.' The effect of the puritan victory on social life is a little obscure. Dorothy Osborne, writing in the earlier fifties, before the rule of the Major Generals, alludes to the ordinary gaieties – race meetings, masques, music, ladies taking their pleasure (masked) in Hyde Park and Spring Garden. But the theatres were closed. Sir Ralph Verney complains (1655) of 'the strange life our youth now lead for want of a court and plays to entertain them.' According to Dorothy, this lack of a court had the worst influence on manners and morals.

> ''Tis strange to see the folly that possesses the young people of this age, and the liberties they take to themselves. I have the charity to believe they appear very much worse than they are, and that the want of a court to govern themselves by is in great part the cause of their ruin. Though that was no perfect school of virtue, yet Vice there wore her mask.'

Whether young people were really worse than usual or not, they certainly had in 'these licentious times' (Ralph Verney again) fewer amusements. Sundays were wretched days, and many prayed for 'a speedy deliverance out of the power of the Major Generals.' According to Royalists, Londoners became very uncivil, and, when not canting and sermonizing, were assaulting the gentry with missiles and rude abuse, while carmen overturned private coaches with cries of 'hell-cart.' 'But these,' comments Evelyn, 'are the natural effects of parity, popular libertinism, and insularly manners.' The overturning of coaches may also have been the natural effect of rivalry, for drivers plying for hire have seldom kindly regarded private cars. Stage coaches also now entered the field, thus increasing the mobility of the masses – another step towards parity. On the other hand, according to the extreme Republicans, Cromwell's swing to the right and his elegant and ceremonious court damaged the cause. It is to be hoped that the young people of the Protectorate found this gay and lavish court a good influence. It was certainly a musical influence; the Protector's tastes not only kept public music in fashion, but allowed the beginning of opera, which was to oust masque. The 'Saints' were dissatisfied with the state of society. Young and old fops still made merry in Hyde Park and Mulberry Gardens, where there walked and drove 'many hundreds of rich coaches and gallants ... most shameful powdered hair men and spotted women.' Evelyn, in 1654, 'observed how the women began to paint themselves, formerly a most ignominious thing, and used only by prostitutes.' (Evelyn was a closer observer of inanimate art than of human beings). Society, though handicapped and irritated, still enjoyed itself, from the Protector down to the rude apprentice and poor peasant.

As to church life, many parsons conformed to the new order, while many sequestered divines still administered the sacraments in the Anglican style. Priests and

CREDULITY, SUPERSTITION, and FANATICISM,
A MEDLEY.

Believe not every Spirit but try the Spirits whether they are of God because many false Prophets are gone out into the World. 1 John 1st. c. 4. V1.

Design'd and Engrav'd by W.m Hogarth.

Published as the Act directs March 5th 15th 1762.

Credulity, Superstition and Fanaticism
– an engraving by William Hogarth, 1762.

congregations taken red-handed at Christmas services were carried off to prison by the military, who 'spake spiteful things of our Lord's Nativity' (soldiers throughout this period were very peculiar). 'The parish churches,' says Evelyn, 'were filled with sectaries of all sorts, blasphemous and ignorant mechanics usurping the pulpits everywhere.' 'Everywhere' is an exaggeration; many incumbents pursued their careers like the Vicar of Bray, not permitting themselves to be thrown out of their stride by the loss of the Prayer Book and the curious new service imposed on them, or even by the rather indecorous behaviour of their congregations. For there were often strange seizures in church, sudden undressings and leapings, spasmodic and piercing cries of devotion and repentance, such as are apt to obtain among devout persons moved beyond endurance by the spirit. Possibly the new drinks went to people's heads, for, though strong liquors were less in vogue, tea, coffee and chocolate began to be drunk, and these, accompanied by ceaseless religious and political discussions, were unsteadying. So was constant newspaper reading, which now became a permanent British vice; in coffee houses they passed the news sheets round, read them out, and passionately debated them. So much sectarian zeal was heating.

According to Anthony à Wood, the Presbyterians and Independents at Oxford were morose, would not enter taverns, but tippled and smoked in their chambers till overcome, and entertained one another there with cheesecakes and tarts. If caught drunk or swearing, they were expelled, so, 'being taken off from these pleasing matters,' they became factious and told tales.

Such, complained Wood and other Royalists, were manners during 'the Interval.' Yet life's normal amenities went on. People idled, joked, sang and played, talked in coffee houses, courted, travelled, consulted astrologers and quacks, hunted witches, met for secret worship, laughed at 'the canters' and their comical ways, wrote verse, read romances, kept journals, drank the waters at Tunbridge and Bath, went by Smithfield and 'saw a miserable creature burning that had murdered her husband,' then on, unperturbed, to see curiosities in ivory.

Still, when the king came back most people were ready enough to 'go just antipodes to the interval time,' and, having a good lead from the court, did so. The theatres were opened and filled and the old plays put on; though Shakespeare and his contemporaries 'began to disgust this refined age,' and new dramatists, considered more refined, took the town by storm. Pepys saw all the plays, and did not mind even being accidentally spat on by the pretty ladies in front of him (apparently play-goers spat backwards, over the shoulder). Other gaieties returned; dancing, cock-fighting, tormenting all sorts of animals in all sorts of delightful ways, masquerades, fireworks, merry feasts; while

Vauxhall opened a new world of enchanting diversions. London was 'a thief to trick you of your purse.' The country gentry, even when 'weary of this deep, dirty country life,' were wiser to stay in it, as, indeed, they usually did. Most serious people agreed with Pepys (who nevertheless put in a pretty merry time himself) that the times were shocking.

> 'At court things are in very ill condition ... and the vices of drinking, swearing, and loose amours, that I know not what will be the end of it. And the clergy so high, that all people that I meet with do protest against their practice. In short, I see no content or satisfaction anywhere.'

All the same, a number of persons had 'a very merry, dancing, drinking, laughing, quaffing and unthinking time,' and probably the height of the clergy left them unperturbed. Pepys liked the village church where, when he entered it with his host, 'at our coming in, the country people all rose with so much reverence,' and the parson began the exhortation 'Right worshipful and dearly beloved.' But all church going was a function of social life; one met neighbours there, ogled beauty, and observed clothes, besides criticizing the sermon.

Patriots complained that people ran after French fashions. 'How charming is the French air, and what an *étourdi bête* is one of our untravelled islanders!' The man of mode, like Sir Fopling Flutter, had French tailors,

Beer Street
– an engraving by William Hogarth, 1750/1.

glovers, wig-makers, scents, and phrases. What patriots had always called French vices were openly the fashion; cuckoldry, always a tedious theme, bid fair to absorb the stage. But in 'the deep dirty country' people went on much the same. They saw nothing there of 'that thin sort of animal that flutters from tavern to playhouse and back again, all his life made of wig and cravat.' Nor of that more intelligent town animal who was entranced by the experiments of the Royal Society. The normal country squire would have been disgusted by one and bored by the other. As to his lady, she might sometimes pine for a little gay life, but disapproved tartly of the outrageous young sparks of both sexes who, she understood, flaunted their ill manners in public places, jested at chastity and jeered at piety. It was not virtue's hour; nor the hour for dignified young women. 'I find our sex is not much valued in our age,' said a lady in 1685, deploring the sex of an infant great niece, 'but before it is a woman I hope they will be better esteemed.' Valued they were, but seldom for reasons which would have pleased Katherine Philips, Lucy Hutchinson, or Mary Astell.

It was not yet the day of the literary salon. Talk and wit centred round the coffee house, the play-house, and wherever men drank together. At the coffee houses, cards 'and the best of conversation till midnight' could be had, ranging from the last court scandal to the state of Europe, from the newest malicious squib to the relative merits of Dryden and Molière. On the whole, and excluding higher moments, conversation was rather spiteful and jokes definitely bawdy, which made neither the less engaging to partakers. Despite the popularity of tea, coffee and chocolate, stronger drinks were not shunned, and deep intoxication often rounded the evening with sleep, unless, rather less deep, it stimulated young gentlemen to run wild through the town. It was a rough and bawdy time. But side by side with immoderate wildness, there was much intellectual curiosity. Virtuosi were fashionable; Charles himself was something of this, unlike his philistine brother, who cared mainly for his mistresses, his navy, and his church.

Class divisions were sharp and arrogant, and religious differences deepened them, now that the Clarendon Code had reclaimed the puritan gentry for the church and made persecuted dissenters of those puritan members of the middle and lower classes who would not be reclaimed. Conventicler-hunting became a new sport for the country magistrate, who pursued it with the zest of revenge. Now that the gentry had deserted the cause, dissent became not only a criminal offence but a low-class one, and the firm alliance of church and gentility began. Whig and Tory gentlemen might attend different coffee houses, but when they sighted a damned conventicler, they gave tongue to the same view hulloo.

EIGHTEENTH CENTURY

THE AUGUSTANS USHERED IN THE NEW CENTURY WITH polish. High living and, if not high thinking, at least incessant talking, prevailed among the more leisured classes. Conversation was ardently pursued; men rose of a morning, met at their pet coffee house, exchanged the news, and talked; later they went to dinner and still talked; then walked and talked in park or Mall, then to assembly or play and talked more, then again to coffee or chocolate house, where they played and talked till midnight. Young law students would arrive at their coffee house in *déshabille* (gay nightcaps, slippers, dressing-gowns and sashes) newspapers in hand, and 'saunter away the time,' admiring one another's get-up; 'the vain things approach each other with an air that shows they regard one another for their vestments.' Later, 'they give place to men who come ... either to transact affairs or enjoy conversation.' The 'affairs' included wagers on current events, such as the arrivals of ships, the terms of treaties, and whether some terrific

Inconveniences of a Crowded Drawing Room
– an engraving by George Cruikshank, 1818.

A magazine sketch from 1878 on the new passion
for the seaside.

noise was an earthquake or a mine exploding. This last bet shocked a clergyman. 'I protest,' he exclaimed, 'they are such an impious set of people that I believe if the last trumpet was to sound, they would bet puppet-show against judgment.'

Each coffee house had its own *clientèle:* some were haunts of fashionable exquisites, some of political discussion, some of literary cliques discussing poetry, art, and one another's reputations, the latest scandals, and the squabbles between poets and their critics.

'Coffee-Houses! the Schools of Politics, of Wit, of polite Learning ... I have always thought that voracious Appetite my Countrymen have after News, to be a particular blessing. Were it not for Newspapers, what would become of herds of fine people, whose Transition from Amusement is constantly to Vice? ... By their assistance we are preserved from degenerating into Brutality, we are softened, civilized, nay, humanized. If a Lady or Gentleman lose their dear Spouses, the whole Nation is taught to grieve in concert with them ... Fires, Executions, Casualties, Deaths, Promotions, etc., are constantly soliciting our Affections of Pity and Joy.'

Thus a journalist of 1721, and never has the case for the popular press been more affectingly put.

Here is a visitor to London in the 1720's:

'We rise by nine, and those that frequent great men's

levees find entertainment at them till eleven ... About twelve the *Beau-Monde* assembles in chocolate and coffee houses ... We are carried to these places in *Sedans* ... If it be fine, we take a turn in the Park till two, when we go to dinner; and if it be dirty you are entertained at picket or basset at *White's,* or you may talk politics at the *Smyrna* and *St. James's* ... but a *Whig* will no more go to the *Cocoa-Tree* ... than a *Tory* will be seen at the *St. James's* ... At two we ... go dine at the Tavern, where we sit till six that we go to the Play, except you are invited to the table of some great man. ... After the play ... to *Tom's* and *Will's* Coffee-Houses, where there is ... picket and the best of conversation till midnight ... Or if you like rather the company of ladies, there are Assemblies at most people of quality's Houses.'

And here is a skit on a young lady's day (1711):

'*From 8 till* 10. Drank two dishes of chocolate in bed, and fell asleep after them. *From* 10 *to* 11. Eat a slice of bread and butter, drank a dish of bohea, read the *Spectator. From* 11 *to* 1. At my toilet, tried a new head. Gave orders for Veny to be combed and washed. *Mem.* I look best in blue. *From* 1 *to* 2.30. Drove to the Change. Cheapened a couple of fans. *Till* 4. At dinner. *Mem.* Mr. Froth passed by in his new liveries. *From* 4 *to* 6. Dressed, paid a visit to old Lady Blithe and her sister ... *From* 6 *to* 11. At basset. *Mem.* Never set again upon the ace of diamonds.'

And so through the week. She ends, 'Looking back into this my journal, I am at a loss to know whether I pass my time well or ill.' Very ill, Miss Hannah More, later in the century, would have said; she was for rational and unrationed conversation and hated idle young women and cards, both its enemies.

In spite of cards and dice, conversation did pretty well. It was said to have become more sparkling; some attributed this coruscation to tea-drinking; for ladies, anyhow, the tea-table became the very centre of gossip. Others thought it might be caused by the variety of odd foods that overseas commerce was bringing to Britain. What with nabobs, spices, nutmeg, parrots, humming-birds, molasses, silks, chocolate, coloured feathers, and little black slaves, the island was assuming an air almost exotic. Rich and rare were the gems people wore; the poor dressed above their station, the rich above any-one's; the citizens aped the gentry, the gentry aped parokeets, and mutual contempt prevailed. Smoking increased; snuff (expensive) became the rage, even among ladies; dining out, complained Defoe, 'over-spreads the face of the nation.' The new rich (some enriched by honest mercantile toil, the spoils of the Indies, or the slave trade, others Bubble-blown), built themselves fine country houses in Islington, famed for its waters and sweet air, in Marylebone ('Many persons arrived in town from their country houses in Mary-lebone,' *The Daily Journal* recorded), Lambeth, Chelsea

A sketch from *The Batchelor's Own Book*
by George Cruikshank.

(where Addison lived among hay-fields) and Stratford, a large village full of little country houses 'for the conveniency of the citizens in summer, where their wives and children generally keep, and their husbands come down on Sundays and return on Mondays.' The country week-end, in fact, had begun; the citizens, by enjoying it, annoyed the gentry who resided near them.

Life for the rich climbed new heights of gaiety; London was a round of diversions – dances, ridottos, routs, masquerades, plays, operas, carnivals at Ranelagh and Vauxhall. Mrs. Montagu, the queen of the Blue-Stockings, was as a girl 'so fond of dancing that I cannot help fancying I was at some time bit by a tarantula.' After dancing all night, one might enjoy a garden breakfast party, with harps and horns imitating birds in the trees, and shelly grottos or Gothic ruins lending romantic fashion to the scene. After breakfast, you might, with Joseph Andrews, take your stick and walk out, carrying a small gentlemanly muff, and saunter till ten, before the day's social round, which was only too liable to end with a party in some chilly grotto after opera or play.

> *The Tavern! Park! Assembly! Mask! and Play!*
> *Those dear destroyers of a tedious day!*
> *That wheel of Fops! That saunter of the Town!*

But there were violent eruptions on society's opulent

The Drunkard's Children, an illustration by George Cruikshank

but unscrubbed face; there were the Hell-Fire Club-
bers, who lived in horrid impiety, died in blasphemy,
ordered 'Holy Ghost Pie' in taverns, and acted plays in
the worst taste about the Virgin Mary; there were
shocking street outrages, Mohocks, bullies, assassins
and robber bands. Society frothed gaily over savage
deeps; while fops sauntered round the town, while wits
and blue-stockings assembled for conversation or
crowded the play-house to damn a new play, while
young ladies patched their faces, spread their fans as
peacocks their tails, and sailed off to mask or rout, while
nabobs built themselves opulent mansions and London
changed its face, while manners grew in elegance, talk in
intelligence, learning and wit, – beneath this charming
structure yawned a dark pit where children were hanged
for theft, men and women publicly and savagely
flogged, pilloried or exposed in stocks, gibbeted in
chains in the streets, left to rot in pestilential gaols for
debt, to starve in filthy cellars, while their betters,
blandly supported by the church, observed that 'gin and
idleness give the poor a riotous and licentious spirit.'

It is pleasant to remember that the poor too had their
pleasures: gin, fairs, public gardens, races, puppet
shows, executions, bear-baitings, the revival meetings
of the brothers Wesley, and later, the educational la-
bours of the sisters More, who, visiting the Cheddar
cottages, 'found each a scene of the greatest ignorance
and vice, the only Bible in the parish being used to prop

a flower-pot.' But on the whole the rich took little interest in the poor, beyond deploring that they dressed above their station (when they could afford to) and showed a riotous and licentious spirit.

It was a violent time; waves of crime swept the country, life and property were at times as unsafe as in the Middle Ages. But society preserved its poise, neither diverted from enjoyment nor shaken in self-satisfaction. Highway robbery was an expected episode on journeys, like the wheel of the coach coming off. More upsetting was earthquake, which sent society fleeing from London, remarking uneasily, 'It's such fine weather, Lord! one can't help going into the country'; so disconcerting were these commotions that quacks sold pills against them to the simple.

On the whole, London society, like its brilliant opposite in Paris, reached, before the menace of the French Revolution alarmed its leaders and sobered its debonairness, a level of intelligent and gregarious urbanity not touched before or since. Not only gentlemen's assemblies but ladies' were intelligent, for the *Bas Bleus* entered the scene, and 'it was much the fashion for several ladies to have evening assemblies, where the fair sex might participate in conversation with literary and ingenious men, animated by a desire to please. These societies were denominated *Blue-Stocking Clubs*.' Thus Boswell, who, however, like his master, occasionally fell out with the Blue Stockings. All the same, they collected

72

An elegant establishment for young ladies
– a water-colour by Edward F. Burney, 1760–1848.

the best company in London; beautiful ladies and intellectual ones alike hung on the words of their dear Dr. Johnson, who enjoyed himself hugely; clever hostesses collected all the candidates for fame, who 'vie with one another till they are as unintelligible as the good folks at Babel,' said the malicious Walpole, who also enjoyed himself there; these parties were indeed, as Hannah More, herself a Blue, remarked, 'such company as it is difficult to find elsewhere.' 'I never invite idiots to my house,' Mrs. Montagu firmly said; and how few, in any age, can make this boast!

So, hooped and caparisoned, plumed, powdered, pig-tailed, fruit and pom-poms piled high on huge coiffures, knee-breeched, snuff-boxed, incomparably conversing, the eighteenth century moved into the Jacobin shadow that flung itself suddenly, intimidatingly, across the Channel. It was the end of an age.

Dandies of the 1820's riding in the row in Hyde Park.

NINETEENTH CENTURY

A NUMBER OF SOBERING EVENTS COMBINED TO DEFLATE the spirits of the *fin-de-siècle* elegants. The Jacobin infection was feared: actually, though riots and dangerous thinking occurred, Britain took it only mildly; but it cramped the style of the old order, as heavy war taxation cramped their purses. Dress simplified; young men resumed the short hair unworn by gentlemen since the Jacobean age. The elderly dandy Horace Walpole was shocked at the 'dirty shirts and shaggy hair' and general slovenliness of the young generation. 'Though gradually undermined and insensibly perishing of atrophy,' said some one, 'dress never totally fell till the era of Jacobinism and of equality, 1791–4.'

You would not have said, attending a party at Holland or Devonshire House at the turn of the century, that dress and fashion were perishing. It was the heyday of the Whig aristocracy and their political salons. Like Mrs. Montagu, they did not ask idiots to their houses, nor suffer fools gladly. Talk ranged over all topics that concerned rational and educated people, and over some (particularly at Devonshire House) others. 'The world' wrote Greville, 'has never seen and never will again see anything like Holland House.' Its guests were even brilliant at breakfast; breakfast parties were one of its main entertainments, and the best talkers in England met there. Rank, high spirits and intelligence still ruled society and politics during the Regency. Not domestic virtue, which was little regarded; nearly every gentleman had his mistress, most married women of fashion their lovers. Much was drunk, much money spilt at cards, dice and prize-fights. Wagering was incessant; it might be on a fight, a cock, a political event, an amorous affair, or the pace of a four-in-hand to Brighton, for driving had become a craze, and young bucks gaily spanked round town and parks in curricles, phaetons or gigs behind fine horses and got up to kill.

Side by side with these pastimes, austere evangelical piety incongruously ran. The sufferings of the poor went less unheeded; even those of bears and bulls were, to the chagrin of the masses, pitied and redressed. Humanitarian societies heightened their agitations against the slave trade; even a few bishops became Abolitionists. In general, a more pious and kindly tone prevailed, though democratic sentiments were suspect. Young radicals got revolution to the head, and thought that bliss was it in that dawn to be alive, but this view was not encouraged, and was regarded as extremely

Promenaders outside the Brighton Pavilion

dangerous when held by the lower orders.

On the whole, poverty was not worse than before, but was often endured under more horrid conditions, as the industrial revolution drove men, women and children to hard labour in factories, mills and mines, while black towns, fed by iron, coal and cotton, sprawled over the country side. The machine age produced a new kind of workman, skilled and independent; a new class of rich, the manufacturers; and a new record of cruel labour for the children of the poor. Scientific agriculture enriched landowners and farmers, but not labourers, pinched by the enclosures and the price of a loaf. Country festivities still flourished, however, and not all the sabbatarianism of the middle classes (increasingly chapel-going) made the Sunday holiday a wholly dull day.

The rich manufacturer gradually superseded the rich merchant as leader of British prosperity. Industry penetrated the governing classes, and the two great parties ceased to be mainly aristocratic. Not that manufacturers were socially accepted in these upper ranks, but vulgar blood, factory-enriched, sapped at the castle walls, and cotton, iron and coal walked the Bath assembly rooms, week-ended at Brighton, and drove smart turn-outs in London's parks. Palladian mansions reared themselves over England, where the radical dissenting manufacturer took root, to come up in the next generation as Tory, Church and Land; still, he could not get into Almack's. A frank snobbery kept each class in place, poised on the shoulders of the class below, blandly trodden by those above. To be a common, ill-bred person, to be neither a gentleman nor a lady, was to be in an outer dimness where individual features were barely distinguishable.

Upper class country society was run by small squires, each on his modest seat. The uncultured, roystering squire Westerns were rare; nineteenth century squires grew to be primmer gentlemen, of greater piety, propriety and culture, often of an evangelical turn, bringing up their children with austere admonitions to virtue and to presenting jelly to the poor. Above them, the reckless, prodigal and free-mouthed aristocracy led their less hampered lives; below them, in the villages and country towns, moved the attorneys, doctors, apothecaries and tradesmen; below these again the great subservient or sullen masses of the poor. The clergy, having steadily mounted, were often now the social equals of the squire, and held down the family living, not always spending much time in it. By their firm attitude towards dissent, they helped to keep religious standards in line with social. They were usually Oxford or Cambridge, and sometimes scholars or antiquarians; zeal they on the whole lacked, and were likeable, comfortable men. 'The English clergy, though upon the whole a very learned, pious, moral and decent set of men, are not very remarkable for professional activity,' as one of them wrote.

The century's first thirty years showed a queerly shot

pattern of flashy luxury, squalid poverty, broad rowdiness, cheerful dissipation, religious piety and elegant propriety. It was an era of pugilism, club life, enchanting new dances, balloon ascents, romantic poetry, fiction and drama. Byron-hunting, and the last Regency beaux. Count D'Orsay succeeded Beau Brummel, Lady Blessington snared literary lions at Gore House, routs became At Homes, ladies flocked to lectures, pressed flowers, made purses of beads and mats of Berlin wool, read the *Keepsake*, and floated round ball-rooms with lovely shoulders sloping up from gowns that passed from classical to puff-sleeved rococo and thence to stately Victorian flow; while gentlemen, progressing from bucks and dandies into swells, curled their hair and grew side whiskers. The portrayed countenances of our ancestors grow more benevolent as the century advances, more pious, less bawdy and less proud. The faces of the poor (which were not portrayed) we picture as more determined than before, more set on rights; or else as patient, emaciated, and liable to be massacred at Peterloo. All classes were better instructed since the days when Miss Hannah More had said, 'I allow no writing for the poor. My object is not to make fanatics, but to train up the lower classes in habits of industry and piety.' Oxford and Cambridge were rising out of the low and unintellectual torpor which had apparently afflicted them for at least a century, the public schools were being Arnoldized, and the elementary schools expanded and improved.

Young ladies were mostly governess-taught; a few by inefficient boarding-schools. Growing up, they stayed (if their parents could support them) at home, where they amused themselves agreeably with parties, visiting, walking, flirting, painting, music, archery (later croquet), riding, helping their mammas in whatever their mammas found tiresome, and their papas if these chanced, as they often did, to be clergymen. Life was not dull, and nor were the young ladies, and certainly not the young gentlemen. Money was not scarce. Houses were being extensively and unbecomingly rebuilt and refurnished. Domestic evenings were cosily gay. When the gentlemen left their wine and cigars to join the ladies, tea was served, at about ten o'clock. There followed cards, paper games, charades, music and conversation, or, in a family circle, reading aloud, before the ladies (who then required more sleep than gentlemen) took their candles and themselves to bed.

In London, life was eased by street gas, hansoms, and more hackney cabs. There were by 1830 also omnibuses; but these were for the lower classes. The rich and smart drove mostly in their own vehicles; hired cabs were dubious, and might be dirty and floored with straw; you never knew who had been in them before you. The streets too were dirty. But gentlemen strolled about them, twirling knobbed canes, promenading Bond Street and the Mall, attending auctions at Christie's, sales at Tattersall's, picture exhibitions, at homes, their clubs, and for a time tea-gardens, but these pleasant haunts became rowdy and ungenteel, and died out one by one. The London poor were reputed to be drunk, degraded, and often dangerous. They had to be kept at arms' length. It was different in the country, where the poor knew their places, and were taken soup, flannel and (when sick) even wine.

The favourite entertainment of rich Londoners was opera. One of the less musically creative of nations, and with the worst natural taste, the cultured British have proved the most rewarding of musical publics, and to succeed in London is to be made. The same paradox obtains in drama: the world's poorest actors (with the possible exception of Red Indians), we have been the most ardent play-goers. For a time the theatre was under a slight evangelical cloud, but this lifted. Meanwhile, since nature demands outlet, a vigorous noise of hymn-singing broke out, and public worship became a community concert.

But the most exciting early Victorian new outlet was dashing about the country in steam trains – just like flying, as the ladies, with their customary lack of ex- actitude, remarked. This form of carriage exercise had royal encouragement; Victoria and Albert and the little ones hugely enjoyed it.

Whether the 'swells' of the forties and fifties were sillier than their dandy, buck, beau and maccaroni ancestors, seems uncertain. To be sure they lisped their r's, saying of the Chartists 'Those dweadful howwid wascals ought to be shot, 'pon my soul'; but each generation of fops has had its jargon – the euphuism of the smart young Elizabethans, the elisions, vowel-corruptions and catch-phrases of the Restoration *beau monde* (Lard! Your laship, let me die, etc.), the broad profanity of Regency bucks, the huntin' and shootin' of late Victorian mashers and Edwardian nuts, all the catch idioms of yesterday and to-day; if any is (as seems probable) foolish, then all are. The Victorian swells were probably, in essence, much as swells have always been.

Ladies seem subject to more change. Female culture was spreading. No longer, in the forties or fifties, was a young woman who read seriously either mocked or admired as a blue-stocking. She might be a lecture addict, discuss the Oxford Movement with Tractarians, Unbelief with doubters, and *In Memoriam* with poetry societies. Did the Thackeray and Dickens meek idiot-angel exist? In the records of our vigorous ancestresses, it is hard to discern her. When, some decades later, female education grew Higher, there was a large feminine public, undaunted by *The Princess*, eager and ready for the upward step.

So comfortable were the upper and middle classes, poised snugly above the dark and smelly swamp of human society, that they could afford to be, and their aspirations led them to be, patrons of art. The Victorians enjoyed pictures and poetry, both good and bad; artists and poets could live (as few can to-day) by their works. Artistic movements made a stir. Some were acclaimed, some execrated, some both; as, for instance, Pre-Raphaelitism, with its undefined, chaotic assortment of execution and aims. Art, music and literature were taken seriously by that prosperous, solid, philistine society which was making England hideous. People believed that the arts mattered, as they believed that religion mattered, and doubt. New prophets, new ideas, were hailed or condemned with serious ardour. Such ideas, such prophets, were the salt of social gatherings.

The æstheticism of the seventies and eighties was this. It stormed society, driving the more advanced to blue china, Morris patterns, lilies, peacock feathers, and trailing gowns, the more reactionary to ribald mockery; unlike any fashion to-day, it made a comic opera. It synchronized with jaeger, and was followed by the nineties, by exquisiteness, the *Yellow Book*, the bicycling craze, violent and rowdy imperialism, the Wagner cult, sailor hats and stiff collars, and an indefinable but apparently recognizable phenomenon in the arts known as 'decadence.'

Women, from the seventies on, went to universities, rowed, played hockey and cricket (they played lawn tennis directly it started, about '75), climbed Alps, travelled abroad alone; became doctors; what was called 'emancipation' had in fact set in. For a time there was a 'new woman,' with all the jokes suitable to such a being; long before the century's end she was no longer new, but part of the landscape.

Walking out in the Seventies.

TWENTIETH CENTURY

Edwardianism cantered in, with an orgy of patriotism, motoring, smart high-life, luxury and zest. It was expensive to keep swimming; week ends grew ever longer, smarter, more extravagant; the reigning monarch, during his pathetically brief and belated run, set a high standard in living, and gilded and animated several continental resorts by his visits, in a manner different from that in which his mother had fashioned the quiet town of Hyères. There was much pleasure, for those who could afford it; life had not been so gay for some time. Nor did society lose its interest in the arts; it chased eagerly after the impressionists, post-impressionists, musical comedy, Shaw at the Court, and later even more eagerly (slightly hampered by hobble skirts) after the dancing Russians. Less fortunate lives meanwhile were raised (they had risen steadily through the last century) by Old Age Pensions, Health Insurance, and mounting wages.

Social life, rudely checked in 1914, for four years had

a military basis; it was a set-back to culture and the arts, for which there was little appetite or time. Marriages became more frequent, hasty and brief; a hectic tension prevailed; people did, as in the next war, fruitless war jobs; others, less fruitless, made fortunes; there was some bitterness between soldiers and the rest.

Peace broke to the noise of thankful rioting, and proceeded for some years to rather the same tune. Interest in the arts returned; the prizes of literature glittered; many more practitioners plucked them. The Russian ballet, exiled now from its native soil by home troubles, became again the fashion. Pictures were exhibited most weeks, and sometimes bought. Travel was resumed, and more people escaped to the continent than ever before. The roads were jammed with cars; cocktails and successive dances crossed the Atlantic; swinging old rhythms gave place to monotonous jogging. Heavier make-up decorated female faces; skirts shortened for a time to the knees; those who valued easy motion were happy in this, but it did not last.

Parties were many and good; more and better, possibly, than in most periods though they have always been rather many and pretty good, owing to human gregariousness. Drinking deepened again among the well-off; among the poor it shallowed, because of closing hours. The sexes more nearly approached one another in this matter, as in other pleasures, than before. Social taboos shifted; some thought this healthy, others not. Anything mentioned among gentlemen could be and was mentioned before and by ladies; Lord Melbourne's 'Now we can talk broad' was outmoded. Young ladies discussed topics of which their mammas had barely (outside literature) heard, or, if they had heard, had not understood, or if they had understood, had never whispered, or, if they had whispered, had blushed. The post-war young ladies, though less addicted to literature, heard, understood, spoke clearly, and did not blush at all; they saw no reason to. Their mammas, infected, soon were doing the same; they told *their* mammas it was the healthy modern spirit. But these old ladies, too old to learn, never got to like it; they remained out of step.

The twenties were, as decades go, a good decade; gay, decorative, intelligent, extravagant, cultured. There were booms in photography, Sunday film and theatre clubs, surrealism, steel furniture, faintly obscure poetry. Proust, James Joyce, dancing, rink skating, large paintings on walls of rooms.

The next decade was more serious, less cultured, less æsthetic, more political. The slump blew like a cold draught at its birth, war stormed like forest fire at its close; between these two catastrophes Communists and Fascists battled and preached, and eyes turned apprehensively across the north sea towards the alarming menace which had leaped up like a strident jack-in-the-box from a beer-cellar to more than a throne. Bets were laid on the date of war. Ivory towers and those who

THE NIGHT SIDE OF FASHION

'The twenties were, as decades go, a good decade;
gay, decorative, intelligent, extravagant, cultured.'

frequented them were under a cloud. People who had never sat on committees before sat on them now; often they were committees for the defence of liberty, democracy, or culture, and culture, losing caste, came to mean anti-Fascism. During these stormy years the Spanish *pronunciamiento* split the British public; the fashionable continental tour was to government or rebel Spain, according to the tourist's political colour.

Tempers ran still higher over the desirability or otherwise of observing international obligations by defending Czechoslovakia. Britain became bomb-conscious: trenches were dug; many Londoners went to earth in the country; hardly had the trenches become water-logged and the earths abandoned than it was all to do again. After that many new fashions came in; windows were criss-crossed with tape; gas masks were carried about and left in cinemas and on blackberry bushes, bags of sand lay on pavements, rotted, sprouted, and burst asunder; through Cimmerian blackness torches were flashed, annoying drivers; women went into trousers, civilians into fire, ambulance and wardens' stations, older men into the Home Guard; young men and women were put into the forces and factories, enemy aliens (hostile and friendly) into camps, British Fascists and others into gaol, policemen into tin hats. Cars crashed all night into street refuges, pedestrians, and each other; the warning banshee wailed by night and day; people left their beds and sat in shelters and knitted Balaclava helmets. Bombs tore homes to pieces; some (if they had survived this catastrophe), took fresh homes, others were surprised to find how well they got on without homes, sleeping in shelters, where a cheerful, if at times malicious, envious and quarrelsome social life throve, continuing even when bomb risk was negligible. Conversation was for some months on catastrophic lines; key words were *siren* (by the less well instructed pronounced sir*een*), *all clear, bomb, under the table, a fine mess in blank street, a nice shelter in dash street,* and *blitz* (believed to be German for air-raid). Provincial social life meanwhile was complicated and somewhat embittered by evacuees from raided cities, whose habits proved often unpleasing to the natives, and refugees from conquered lands, who also did not invariably give satisfaction to patriots. In these areas, conversation tended to turn on the attributes and practices of one or other of these two groups. Also, and in all areas, on food: what was permitted, what was to be had, what was not permitted and where this was to be had and at what cost, what was not to be had at all and how so-and-so had had it. When bombs were not descending, or ruins being searched for household goods before the demolition men could get at them, food talk often beat bomb talk. So, later, did clothes coupons talk (those who said sir*een* said *cyoopons*). Standards of smartness depreciated, to the relief of those who found them tedious or inaccessible. Bare legs became a feminine summer fashion; men, more sartorially conservative, clung to such socks as they had. Evening dress was seldom seen. Life was less decorative and less social; but human gregariousness found, as always, its outlets. For many, indeed, it became more communal than before; uniformed men and women were assembled for military or civil defence, and, in the intervals of their duties, played, ate and drank together; it was a life which tended to resolve class distinctions; taxi-drivers, dustmen, window-cleaners (this profession had naturally languished), shop assistants, hairdressers, and young ladies and gentlemen from expensive schools and universities, met and played and worked on level terms, addressing each other by nicknames. English social life is, in these curious, dark, troubled years, moving a few steps nearer that democracy for which we say we are fighting and have never yet had. Only a few steps; and whether these will be retraced or continued when the solvent furnace of war dies down, and we are left to grope a way through wreckage and smouldering ashes, we cannot yet know.

Rose Macaulay, 1942

ACKNOWLEDGMENTS

PRION have endeavoured to observe the legal requirements with regard to the rights of suppliers of illustrative material and would like to thank **Mary Evans Picture Library**, the **Mansell Collection** and the **Dover Pictorial Archive** for their generous assistance. *An Elegant Establishment of Young Ladies*, a water colour by Edward F. Burney (1760-1848) is reproduced courtesy of the **Victoria & Albert Museum**.